In Dreams
I Run Wildly

In Dreams
I Run Wildly

Edited by Lucy Duckworth

On November 4th 1999, Nyaru Mentang opened its gates to the first orphans rescued from the illegal pet trade. Eleven years on, and while we may celebrate the many hundreds of lives Lone Dröscher Nielsen and the Borneo Orangutan Survival Foundation have saved, the celebration is tinged with sadness, that such a place need exist at all.

Substitute mother to orangutans. That is probably the most fitting way to describe a woman who has become known around the world as "The Great Dane". Her name is Lone Dröscher Nielsen and she has dedicated the last 18 years of her life to saving the orangutan from extinction. Founder and Manager of the Nyaru Mentang Sanctuary, she heads the rescue operations to save orangutans that would otherwise not have the chance of survival; orphaned babies whose mothers have been killed, and adult orangutans that have lost their home to the destruction of the rainforest by Man. They stay at the centre, safe and cared for, until they can be released into the wild.

Who are we?

We are the Borneo Orangutan Survival Foundation, a charity dedicated to saving orangutans from extinction and protecting its rainforest home.

What do we do?

We are responsible for the rescue and rehabilitation of hundreds of wild and orphaned orangutans, who have been displaced by the relentless devastation of their rainforest home for palm oil production. If these young orangutans are not killed, they are sold into the illegal pet trade.

Why do we do it?

We do it because of the faces you see on these pages. These are the innocent victims. They have lost their mothers, their homes and their resources.

So what can YOU do to help save the species?

We rely entirely on donations to continue our work and achieve our goal - to rehabilitate and prepare these orangutans for a life in the wild and ultimately return them to their wild rainforest home.

With your help, we can show everyone that this beautiful area of the world and its red-haired inhabitants are an invaluable part of the planet we share.

To lie on a branch
High above the jungle floor
What is more perfect?

Anonymous

The tools of my trade
are found in fingers
and feet
Often the two meet.

Anonymous

I want to sleep –
Swat the flies
Softly, please.

Masaoka Shiki

Why harm or slaughter
such intelligent bright life?
Big, gentle brown eyes.

Helen Albea

First autumn morning
the mirror I stare into
shows my father's face.

Murakami

Under this bright moon
I sit like an old Buddha
knees spread wide.

Yoshi Mikami Issa

Will you turn toward me?
I am lonely too,
this autumn evening.

Matsuo Basho

Nature can feed me
But my world is now
cut down
Where is my freedom?

Maggie Zwaan

Come with me,
Let's play together, sparrow
without a mother.

Kobayashi Issa

Their deep brown eyes yearn,
A silent voice wants to cry;
Please let me go home.

Matthew Rooke

Mother and baby
Be as nature intended
Living wild and free.

Helene Sterzl

Long arms and legs stretched
Soulful eyes staring at me
Offer only love.

Lucy Smith

I sink my teeth
into a ripe persimmon—
it dribbles down my beard.

Masaoka Shiki

Won't you come
    and see loneliness?
Just one leaf
    from the kiri tree.

Matsuo Basho

Riding the wide leaf
of the banana tree,
the tree frog clings.

Kikaku

Fallen sick on a journey,
In dreams I run wildly
Over a withered moor.

Matsuo Basho

Loving families.
Playing, climbing, nurturing,
free orangutans.

Heather Bradley

I wonder in what fields today
He chases dragonflies in play
My little boy who ran away.

Kaga no Chiyo

Sparkly hopeful eyes
Scream in need of protection
Thankful for being heard.

Sharon Kahan

Shall we ever see
the time your reign brings
    lasting peace
to all hills and streams.

Iio Sogi

Here it stands in awe,
A wonderful tree of might,
I rest here a while.

Anonymous

Passing through the
world
Indeed this is just a
shelter from the rain.

Iio Shogi

A picture says a
thousand words but it hides
a million heartaches.

Wendy Young

Now I see her face
The old woman, abandoned
the moon her only
    companion.

Matsuo Basho

There's no need to speak,
And no need to wonder why
Life is what it is.

Anonymous

Red flash in the green dapple
Many kin and kith long lost,
Swing free forever.

Carolyn Davies

Oh! Ginger baby
Funny, fuzzy and clever,
Looking forward with
     hope.

Philippa Hunt

The moment two
    bubbles are united,
they both vanish.
A lotus blooms.

Kigo Murakami

So sad it is to
see lovely orangutans
without their mothers.

Emma Lokuciejewski

The Old Man of the Trees
His perch is dwindling
yet hope springs eternal.

Oliver Segal

As the great old trees are
marked for felling,
    the birds
build their new spring nests.

Yoshi Mikami Issa

Trees are less
    each year for us.
I am a giant ~
But I fear you more.

Emma Benton

To have tomorrows
we must save wildlife
today
from man's ignorance.

Mags Holdsworth

A faint yellow rose
almost hidden in deep grass.
And then it moves.

Yoshi Mikami Issa

I like to eat fruit.
My favourites: rambutan,
durian, and figs.

Matthew Rooke

Now the swinging bridge
is quieted with creepers.
Like our tendrilled life.

Matsuo Basho

Picture credits

Many thanks to those who kindly donated their pictures to this book.

In Dreams I Run Wildly
978-19061-81079

Published by Bound Originals on behalf of Borneo Orangutan Survival UK
BOS UK • 8 Temple Square • Aylesbury • HP20 2QH • United Kingdom
www.savetheorangutan.co.uk
Registered Charity No. 1099591

www.boundoriginals.co.uk
Tithe Barn • Clouts Farm • Ide Hill Road • Bough Beech • Kent • TN8 7PH

For Polly Diana - my own little red-haired baby.

10 9 8 7 6 5 4 3 2 1
1st Edition
Printed in Slovenia